NORTH WESSEX DIESELS

KEVIN SMITH

AMBERLEY

First published 2020

Amberley Publishing
The Hill, Stroud
Gloucestershire, GL5 4EP

www.amberley-books.com

Copyright © Kevin Smith, 2020

The right of Kevin Smith to be identified as
the Author of this work has been asserted in
accordance with the Copyrights, Designs and
Patents Act 1988.

ISBN 978 1 4456 9382 8 (print)
ISBN 978 1 4456 9383 5 (ebook)

British Library Cataloguing in Publication Data.
A catalogue record for this book is available from
the British Library.

Typesetting by Aura Technology and Software
Services, India. Printed in the UK.

Introduction

Wessex was a region in author Thomas Hardy's novels and poems, named after the medieval Anglo-Saxon kingdom. Although Hardy's Wessex was fictional, it was based on reality, with the towns and villages of the area given alternative names. The fictional Wessex consisted of several regions, one of which was North Wessex. In more recent times the name North Wessex Downs has been adopted to define an Area of Outstanding Natural Beauty that includes better-known geographical features such as the Berkshire Downs, the Marlborough Downs and the Vale of Pewsey.

This is an illustrated record of the main line railways in and around the North Wessex area during the fifteen years between 2004 and 2019. The region covered stretches from Reading in the east to beyond Swindon and Pewsey in the west, reaching Oxford in the north and Basingstoke in the south. The backdrop is predominantly rural, featuring gently rolling countryside, although there is some surviving line-side industry. The period covered preceded great change on the railways, arguably the greatest in the region since the abolition of Brunel's ill-fated broad gauge. In recent years much of the infrastructure has been altered significantly with the installation of overhead electrification equipment for the new Great Western Railway Inter-City Express Trains. These have replaced the much-loved Inter-City 125 high-speed trains, which have given over forty years of front-line express passenger service in the region and have become an icon of the diesel era on Britain's railways.

The author first visited the North Wessex area during the mid-1980s, whilst following the British Rail English Electric-built Class 50 locomotives, which operated many of the remaining loco-hauled express services to and from London's Paddington and Waterloo stations. It wasn't until moving to the area in the late 1990s, and the advent of high-quality digital cameras during the early 2000s, that the author began to record the local railway scene. By then the railway had been privatised and many of the British-built locomotives had been retired from service, although some were to reappear working for numerous small operators, with varying degrees of business success.

During the period covered, imported locomotives have dominated the rail freight scene. BR had dabbled in outsourcing locomotive construction to overseas builders during the 1970s, however the early members of Class 56 were essentially still British locomotives, despite being built in Romania. The use of imported locomotives on the British network really began when Foster Yeoman ordered new heavy freight machines from General Motors. These worked the highly demanding aggregate flows from their Merehead Quarry in the Mendips to various destinations in the south and south-east of England. Introduced during 1986 and designated Class 59, these locomotives were to have a profound impact on the shape of things to come on the privatised railway. Just over a decade later, when new private operator English, Welsh and Scottish Railway ordered 250 diesel-electrics from GM they were constructed using a very similar bodyshell design to the 59s. Known as Class 66, these locomotives quickly swelled in numbers as other operators followed the EWS lead. Subsequently many other types of locomotive and rolling stock for the British railway network have been built or designed overseas.

The photographs contained within have been selected to give an account of the varied types of diesel-powered trains and their operators' liveries. The vast majority of traffic in the area conveys passengers, however for increased variety most of the images depict freight workings. The latter includes aggregates from the Mendips, South Wales steel, coal, cement, oil, bitumen, china clay, automotive, freightliners, refuse, fly ash, MOD and infrastructure trains. The classes of locomotive and multiple unit represented are 08, 31, 33, 37, 43, 47, 50, 52, 56, 57, 59, 60, 66, 67, 68, 70, 150, 165, 166, 180, 220 and 221.

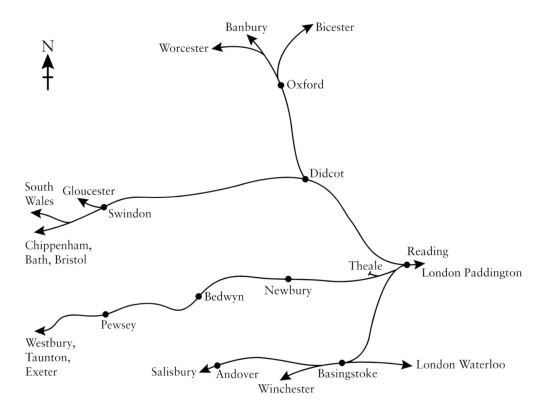

The Inter-City 125s, or HSTs, are arguably the best trains to have operated on the British network. After more than forty years, 2019 saw the end of scheduled HST services to and from London Paddington. Wearing the popular Inter-City 'swallow' heritage livery of the late BR era, No. 43185 *Great Western* passes Hungerford Common, at the head of the 09.00 Penzance to Paddington, on 20 April 2019. This train, and an equivalent Down working, were branded 'The Cornish Riviera Express', a name introduced by the Great Western Railway in 1904. HSTs took over this duty from locomotive-hauled stock during 1979–1980, setting an impressive record for longevity of service, having been incumbent for longer than any other type of motive power in the train's 115-year history.

Two weeks after the last service trains ran, 1 June 2019 saw a farewell tour for full-length Great Western Railway HSTs. The first production power car No. 43002 passes Didcot North Junction whilst leading the second leg of the tour: the 07.37 London Paddington to Carmarthen via Hereford. Last-built power car No. 43198 was at the rear of the formation. Earlier the tour had run from Bristol Temple Meads to Paddington and later it returned to London via Swansea, Gloucester and Swindon before a final trip to Plymouth.

The new order: The Hitachi class 800 and 802 Inter-City Express Trains have taken over the long-distance services to and from London Paddington. These bimodal units are able to take electrical power from overhead lines or from on-board diesel-powered generators. On a very pleasant spring evening an unidentified nine-car unit heads west beside the Kennet & Avon Canal near Kintbury on 10 April 2019.

Turning the clock back to the late 1980s, Old Oak Common allocated Class 50 No. 50031 *Hood* stands at Reading's platform 4, having arrived with the 13.17 Paddington to Oxford on 26 March 1988. The platform canopies seen here were swept away with major rebuilding and expansion of the station, which was completed during 2014.

On 20 July 1989 Network SouthEast-liveried Class 50 No. 50025 *Invincible* calls at Oxford with the 11.18 York to London Paddington Inter-City service, whilst construction of the current station building was in progress. By summer 1989 the division of British Rail into business sectors was well under way and the corporate BR blue was rapidly giving way to a wide variety of liveries.

A remarkable survivor from the British Rail era was the livery carried by class 60 No. 60054 *Charles Babbage*. The locomotive is illustrated during 2007 still wearing the original Trainload Freight petroleum sector markings it carried from new in 1991, albeit somewhat work-stained and without cast BR double arrows or shed plates. On 17 March this stalwart was captured at Bourton near Swindon whilst, appropriately, working the Theale to Margam empty oil tanks.

Over the years new freight operators have emerged, some bringing withdrawn locomotives originating from the BR era back to main line service. Here Colas Rail Freight Class 56 Nos. 56078 and 56096 pass Ruffinswick Farm near Compton Beauchamp in glorious late autumn light, with empty covered steel wagons en route from Tilbury, east of London, to Llanwern in South Wales on 6 December 2014.

10 September 2006 and British Railways two-tone green extended-range Class 47/4 No. 47812 approaches Cholsey on the Up main with the 15.30 Cardiff Canton to Old Oak Common empty stock move. The locomotive was in the ownership of Riviera Trains Limited, a spot hire company providing locomotives and stock for charters and train operating companies.

In 1986 Class 59/0 No. 59001 *Yeoman Endeavour* was the first of the now ubiquitous General Motors-built diesel-electric locomotives to arrive in the UK. This particular locomotive and its classmates have had a long association with the North Wessex area, concentrated on aggregate trains from the Mendips. Just over twenty years after introduction the pioneer is seen working a train of empty Foster Yeoman bogie hoppers from Theale to Merehead Quarry. The location is Manningford, just west of Pewsey, on 13 March 2007.

Love them or hate them, during the last twenty years the imported Class 66s have proved their reliability and versatility, being used on a variety of freight traffic and much lighter duties such as this rail-head treatment train. Seen approaching Little Bedwyn, not long before sunset on 2 November 2016, are locomotives Nos. 66031 and 66096.

Freightliner was the second operator to acquire Class 66s, initially to replace Class 47s on intermodal traffic. Since the introduction of the 66s the operator has diversified into other freight flows including aggregates. Class 66/5 No. 66585 passes Froxfield Bottom Lock, on the Berks & Hants line, whilst working the 08.28 Cardiff Pengam to Theale loaded aggregates on 27 March 2012.

The last main line diesel locomotive to be constructed for British Rail was Class 60 No. 60100, which emerged from the Brush factory at Loughborough in 1992. Well liked by train crews and enthusiasts, following privatisation, Class 60 has had mixed fortunes, but happily examples are still in traffic today having undergone major overhaul. Seen passing Hungerford Marsh on 19 April 2007, No. 60100 *Pride of Acton* in EWS livery heads a uniform rake of JHA Yeoman bogie hoppers forming a mid-morning departure from Merehead Quarry to Acton Yard.

The Class 165 and 166 'Turbo' units were also survivors from the BR era, now replaced on electrified lines by new Class 387 EMUs. Two-car No. 165130 is reflected in the Kennet & Avon Canal near Froxfield on 15 April 2007. The unit is wearing the livery of the former Thames Trains operating company, which had taken over services from Network SouthEast when the railway was privatised. In 2004 First Group took over operation of these services from Thames Trains and the units were adorned with First Great Western Link branding, as seen here. During 2006 this franchise was combined with the Great Western and Wessex Trains franchises to form the Greater Western franchise.

At the time of writing the Mendip stone contract with DB was due to end during November 2019. The new operator, Freightliner, had agreed to purchase the eight Mendip Rail Class 59s. However, the fate of DB's own Class 59/2s was not clear. No. 59205 has just passed Crofton crossing with empty Mendip Rail wagons from Acton Yard to Merehead Quarry during the late afternoon of 31 March 2015.

The closure of Didcot A Power Station in March 2013 was a significant event in the area, bringing an end to the coal and oil trains that once fed the four 500 megawatt generating units. Approximately seven years before closure No. 66106 leaves the coal sidings with empty HTA wagons bound for Avonmouth on 5 April 2006.

The Berks & Hants Railway consisted of two branches from Reading, the first going to Hungerford the other diverging at Southcote Junction to reach Basingstoke. The Hungerford line was later extended to Devizes and the majority of the extension now forms part of a through route to Westbury and the south-west of England. This line is still generally referred to as the Berks & Hants. Class 59/0 No. 59002 *Alan J Day* comes off the Westbury line at Southcote Junction with the 07.12 Merehead Quarry to Acton Yard aggregates train on 20 April 2016. This train is timed for a maximum speed of 45 mph and is scheduled to arrive in the Reading area after the morning peak.

On 30 November 2016 Class 37/4 No. 37421 leads the 06.43 Tyseley to Bristol test train towards Theale Loop, passing Burghfield Road, Southcote, on the outskirts of Reading. No. D6967 was built in 1965 at the English Electric Vulcan Foundry and became 37267 under TOPS. The locomotive was refurbished and fitted with electric train supply at Crewe Works during 1985 and emerged as No. 37421. No. 37219 can be seen at the rear of the formation.

Freight on the Berks & Hants is dominated by aggregates traffic mainly originating from Merehead and Whatley Quarries in the Mendips. The sidings at Theale received aggregates and other regular flows of cement from Earles Sidings near Hope in Derbyshire, sand from Grain in Kent and oil from Robeston in South West Wales and Lindsey refinery in Lincolnshire. Signs of spring are evident in this view of No. 60017 approaching Burghfield Road, Southcote, at the start of its journey with the Theale to Margam empty Murco oil tanks on Saturday 20 April 2013.

There are four separate freight terminals at Theale, two of which receive aggregates and are equipped with hopper discharge facilities. One receives aggregates from Merehead Quarry and is still known as Theale Foster Yeoman. The other is served by Whatley Quarry and is referred to as Theale ARC. There are also sidings serving the Murco oil depot and the Lafarge cement terminal. The author was grateful to be given access to private land on the south side of the line to photograph trains using the sidings. No. 66172 has just arrived with the 09.10 departure from Acton Yard on 27 May 2015. Having run around it is pushing back into the ARC siding, ready for unloading using the under track conveyor.

On 3 June 2015, the former Bardon-liveried No. 66623 *Bill Bolsover* waits to leave the Lafarge cement siding at Theale with the 11.13 departure of discharged tanks, for Earles Sidings at Hope. Note the use of two-axle wagons, whereas by this time the vast majority of freight services in the area employed high-capacity bogie vehicles. To the left of the train is the Foster Yeoman aggregates siding with its hopper discharge facilities. To the right is the cripples siding, providing refuge to a single bogie hopper wagon that requires attention.

Engineering work often requires services to be diverted from their usual route, providing some interesting opportunities for railway photographers. This was the case on 21 February 2015 when No. 60019 *Port of Grimsby & Immingham* was captured leaving the west end of the yard at Theale with the 11.27 departure, formed of empty Murco tanks, bound for Margam in South Wales. The oil empties normally leave Theale in the opposite direction, routed via Didcot, Swindon and Bristol Parkway. However, this day was one of many during 2015 when Great Western main line electrification work necessitated diversion of this train via Newbury, Westbury and Bath.

At Padworth we get our first glimpse of a waterway that forms part of an inland link between London and Bristol. Here it is known as the Kennet Navigation, where the natural course of the River Kennet is supplemented by engineered channels to allow the passage of boats. To the west, at Newbury, the waterway joins to the Kennet & Avon Canal. Class 59/1 No. 59104 *Village of Great Elm* passes with the 07.12 Merehead Quarry to Acton Yard aggregates, formed of an almost uniform set of Yeoman hoppers, on 23 August 2016.

Just to the west of Theale is Towney Down loop, which rejoins the main line at Padworth. After allowing passenger trains to pass, GBRf Class 66 No. 66750 *Bristol Panel Signal Box* leaves the loop with empty aggregate wagons from Wellingborough to Whatley Quarry. The line on the right is now disused but once served sidings near Aldermaston station, which included an oil depot.

The Class 67s were originally intended to work mail trains on the unelectrified part of the network. However, with the loss of the contract with Royal Mail during 2003, the locomotives have found employment on other workings, including charters such as this one. No. 67025 *Western Star* approaches Frouds Lane, Aldermaston, at the head of the 09.53 London Victoria to Cardiff Central rugby extra on 14 February 2009. This stretch of line was once the site of water troughs, which were used by steam locomotives to replenish their water tanks whilst on the move.

Scrap concrete sleepers are on their way to Peterborough from Taunton's Fairwater Yard behind GBRf Class 66 No. 66703 *Doncaster Power Signal Box 1981–2002*. The train is caught as it approaches Frouds Lane on the crisp and bright morning of 9 March 2007. In the author's opinion this is the most attractive livery to have adorned this class of locomotive.

Present-day passenger services on the Berks & Hants are a mixture of longer distance and local workings. Generally there is roughly an hourly service between London and Plymouth, with half of these trains extended to and from Penzance. The local services run between Reading and Newbury and London and Bedwyn. Passing former gravel pits near Woolhampton on 22 March 2015 is No. 43041 at the head of the 12.57 London Paddington to Penzance.

On 30 November 2011 Direct Rail Services Class 37 No. 37604 approaches Brimpton Road at the head of a westbound Network Rail test train. The locomotive was a product of the English Electric Vulcan Foundry during 1960 as D6707. During 1974 it became No. 37007 under TOPS and was renumbered again as No. 37506 after heavy general overhaul at Crewe, emerging in 1986. In 1995 it was selected to work for European Passenger Services, when it also gained its current number.

After the introduction of multiple aspect signalling during 1978, the former Colthrop Sidings Box, now named Colthrop Crossing, was retained to control the road crossing seen here and also those at Thatcham and Midgham. No. 43176 passes on 7 March 2015 at the head of the 11.33 Exeter St David's to London Paddington.

On 14 December 2016 there are signs of the forthcoming electrification of the line as No. 66040 passes Newbury Racecourse with the 10.37 Whatley to Hayes aggregates hoppers. The backdrop of light industry is quite typical of much of the line between Reading and Newbury, in contrast to the more rural landscapes further west.

First Great Western Class 57 No. 57603 *Tintagel Castle* makes an unusual daylight appearance at Newbury whilst working the empty sleeper stock from Penzance to Old Oak Common on 15 July 2013. The previous night's Up Night Riviera had failed, necessitating this balancing stock move. (Photograph by Richard Sulzmann)

Newbury station is the setting for Class 67 No. 67030 as it passes on the Up through line with an Exeter St David's to London Paddington football extra, on 20 May 2007. The first five coaches are Anglia liveried mark two stock, including a DBSO immediately behind the locomotive. First Great Western Link-liveried Class 165 No. 165137 rests in the bay platform. The GWR station footbridge seen here has since been removed.

Overhead electrification equipment has been installed as far as Newbury, and Class 387 EMUs now operate services from London and Reading that terminate here. However, DMUs were still used on the services continuing to Bedwyn. The longer distance services hung on to HSTs longer than the other routes from Paddington, but since the May 2019 timetable change all diagrams have been operated by IETs. HST power car No. 43196 heads the 13.05 London Paddington to Plymouth at speed on the Down main at Newbury on 1 October 2015. At the time the forthcoming electrification was hardly in evidence and Newbury station retained much of its Great Western Railway character.

In recent years the six EWS/DB-owned Class 59/2s were concentrated on Mendip stone traffic, used alongside the eight Mendip Rail Class 59/0 and 59/1 locomotives. Leaving Newbury on 7 September 2012, Class 59/2 No. 59204 has just passed the site of Enborne Junction, where the Didcot, Newbury & Southampton Railway diverged heading southwards to join the London & South Western Railway at Shawford Junction. The train is the 12.40 Acton Yard to Merehead, consisting mainly of empty box wagons.

No. 43163 leads a London Paddington-bound express at Kintbury on 6 March 2009. The waterlogged wooded landscape seen here, known as carr, is typical of the area surrounding the River Kennet and the railway.

A colourful scene during the afternoon of 23 August 2016. Hanson-liveried Class 59/1 No. 59103 *Village of Mells* waits at signal TR849 at the eastern end Hungerford Up loop whilst heading the 11.42 Merehead Quarry to Theale loaded stone train. Passing on the Down line is Class 59/2 No. 59201 with the 12.40 Acton to Merehead empties. The Class 59/2s were originally built for National Power for use on coal and limestone trains, but ownership was taken over by EWS during 1998 and then passed to DB. Since 2005 they have supplemented the pool of Mendip Rail Class 59/0 and 59/1 locomotives working from Merehead and Whatley Quarries.

The British-built Class 60 locomotives were also frequent performers on Mendip stone traffic, although they have been less common in recent years. In a very lucky burst of sunshine, recently overhauled DB Schenker Class 60 No. 60019 passes Hungerford Up loop with the 10.37 Whatley to St Pancras loaded aggregates train.

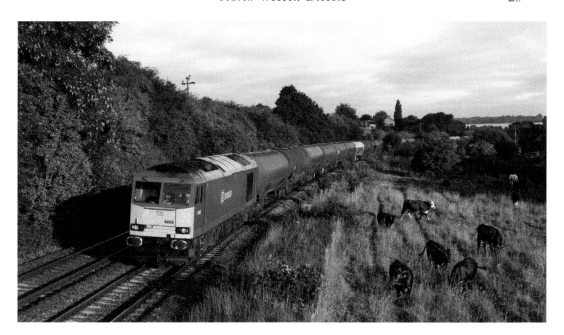

Another working that regularly employs Class 60s is the flow of oil from Robeston in South West Wales to Theale. This is a challenging train to photograph on its normal path, running overnight and reaching its destination early in the morning. However, on 17 July 2014 a thirty-minute delay worked in the photographer's favour, allowing the shadows to clear from the line at Hungerford Common before No. 60020 passed at 06.25.

7 March 2016 produced ideal photographic conditions with excellent visibility. In the early afternoon No. 66107 was caught heading the 10.37 Whatley to Churchyard Sidings as it crossed Hungerford Common. The Kennet & Avon Canal is clearly visible and Hungerford station can just be seen near the back of the train.

On 10 March 2015 Class 166 DMU No. 166217 gets away from its stop at Hungerford station, forming the 12.38 Bedwyn to London Paddington. The former siding seen here has since been lifted. Hungerford was the original terminus of the Berks & Hants Railway. Construction of the Berks & Hants Extension Railway took the line beyond here, originally to Devizes.

For over thirty years Class 59s have had charge of a large proportion of the aggregate workings from the Mendips. Between 1993 and 2019 the Class 59/0s and Class 59/1s were managed by Mendip Rail, a joint venture between the rail operating divisions of Aggregate Industries (formerly Foster Yeoman) and Hanson Aggregates (formerly ARC) intended to improve the efficiency of rail operations from the quarries. Yeoman-liveried Class 59/0 No. 59002 *Alan J Day* passes Hungerford Marsh with loaded hoppers from Merehead to Acton Yard on 21 October 2008. During this period Freightliner hoppers were hired to supplement the Mendip Rail wagon fleet, providing some welcome variety for photographers.

The 07.12 Merehead to Acton Yard often conveys two or three portions destined for different receiving terminals in the south-east of England. In this view taken on 2 March 2009 at least two portions are visible, with open box wagons followed by hoppers. The train, led by EWS-liveried Class 59/2 No. 59204 *Vale of Glamorgan*, is making steady progress as it passes Froxfield.

A glimpse of Aggregate Industries-liveried Class 59/0 No. 59001 *Yeoman Endeavour* and its train seen from the towpath of the Kennet & Avon Canal at Froxfield on 6 March 2009. The locomotive was the first built of the now familiar General Motors bodyshell design that arrived in the UK at Southampton during January 1986.

Froxfield Bottom Lock is the location for this view of Yeoman-liveried Class 59/0 No. 59004 *Paul A. Hammond* and matching wagons forming the 07.12 Merehead to Acton Yard on 23 May 2012. To gain some extra height the photographer remembers balancing atop steps placed rather precariously on the lock gates, a rather risky practice that is not necessary now with the advent of photographic poles.

On 28 February 2005 a heavy overnight frost had frozen the Kennet & Avon Canal at Froxfield between Hungerford and Bedwyn. The ice had yet to thaw when D1015 *Western Champion* passed with the 07.40 London Victoria to Paignton Past Time Rail excursion 'The Staite Pullman'. No. D1015 worked the train as far as Taunton, where GWR steam locomotives No. 6024 *King Edward I* and No. 7082 *Bradley Manor* took it forward to Paignton.

Skirting the northern bank of the Kennet & Avon Canal between Hungerford and Bedwyn is No. 59201 at the head of the 15.24 departure from Acton Yard to Merehead Quarry on 9 April 2016. Well-lit photography from the northern side of the Berks & Hants line is limited to the longer evenings of the late spring and summer months and, as in this case, there is often a balance to be struck between favourable light angles and lengthening shadows.

An unidentified London-bound HST catches the last golden rays before sunset near Little Bedwyn on 3 December 2008.

2016 marked the fortieth anniversary of the introduction of the first production HST power car, No. 43002. To celebrate it was returned to the 1970s blue, grey and yellow livery with Inter-City 125 branding, and named *Sir Kenneth Grange* after the inventor of this iconic design. Here the power car leads the 18.02 London Paddington to Penzance as it approaches Little Bedwyn, passing the former crossing keeper's house at Fore Bridge, on 24 May 2016.

Stations between Newbury and Bedwyn were mainly served by Class 165 or 166 'Turbo' units. Nearing journey's end, No. 166213 passes the picturesque village of Little Bedwyn and St Michael's Church, forming the 09.18 London Paddington to Bedwyn service on 2 November 2016. Here the railway separates the River Dun from the canal. The footbridges, which span all three, are on the site of a former road crossing.

GBRf Class 66 No. 66707 passes Little Bedwyn with scrap concrete sleepers heading to Peterborough for disposal on 21 April 2009. The sleepers will have come from various work sites, having first been taken to the high output operations base at Taunton Fairwater Yard before forming this block train, which at the time was a regular sight on the Berks & Hants route.

FM Rail Class 47/7 No. 47712 *Artemis*, in Blue Pullman livery, heads matching coaching stock towards Little Bedwyn during the long summer evening of 1 July 2006. The train is returning to London Paddington after a day trip to Paignton. Type 4 No. D1948 was built at Brush Traction at Loughborough in 1966 and was renumbered 47505 under TOPS. During 1979 the locomotive was the last of the original twelve Class 47s selected for fitting with push-pull equipment for use on Scottish services, initially between Glasgow and Edinburgh, and was renumbered 47712.

The dark green of the Great Western Railway franchise can be challenging to photograph, winter months offering the best opportunities with the sun lower in the sky and the muted tones of vegetation. Here the first HST set to be re-liveried, led by No. 43188, is seen between Little Bedwyn and Great Bedwyn whilst working the 09.06 London Paddington to Plymouth on 24 February 2016.

During the evening of Saturday 6 June 2015 a small group of passengers wait for the London Paddington train at Bedwyn while No. 66031 passes with the 14.35 Churchyard Sidings to Westbury empty hoppers. During 2019 all passenger services calling here either terminated or originated at Bedwyn, with the exception of two early morning Up trains and three Down services in the evenings Monday to Friday.

Class 166 No. 166221 pulls into the turn-back siding at Bedwyn, provided for terminating services from London Paddington, Newbury and Reading. The station's Up platform can be glimpsed through the road bridge on 27 June 2011.

Since this view was captured on 19 May 2014 the Bedwyn turn-back siding has been lengthened and the foot crossing moved slightly further west to accommodate five-car IETs. Empty aggregate wagons from Acton Yard pass during the early evening headed by a mixed pair, Class 66/0 No. 66069 and Class 59/2 No. 59206.

2016 saw the thirtieth anniversary of the arrival of the first General Motors Class 59, and to commemorate Class 59/0 locomotives were branded with commemorative artwork proclaiming '30 years – Class 59'. On 19 June 2017 No. 59004 *Paul A. Hammond* approaches Bedwyn station with the 07.20 Merehead to Acton Yard loaded aggregates wagons.

On 28 February 2005 an unidentified HST passes Great Bedwyn en route from London Paddington to the West Country. This view was taken from the Bedwyn to Wilton road looking towards Bedwyn station and shows St Mary's Church.

Hanson Class 59/1 No. 59102 *Village of Chantry* approaches Bedwyn with the morning Merehead to Acton Yard aggregates train on 29 June 2011. Visible on the disused bridge are anti-tank cylinders that formed part of a Second World War defensive line called GHQ Stop Line Blue. These defences were positioned along the Kennet & Avon Canal to hinder an invasion.

On 19 March 2006 FM Rail Class 47/7 No. 47703 *Hermes* is seen between Bedwyn and Crofton with a rather mixed rake of BR Mk 1 stock, en route from Old Oak Common to Bishops Lydeard on the West Somerset Railway. The locomotive is wearing the livery of Fragonset Railways, a spot hire company formed in 1997. The company merged with Merlin Rail in January 2005 to form FM Rail, which lasted until December 2006 when administrators were appointed.

EWS-liveried Class 59/2 No. 59203 *Vale of Pickering* works the morning train of empties from Theale Foster Yeoman to Merehead Quarry, seen between Bedwyn and Crofton on a perfect spring morning on 19 April 2007.

Although they can weigh in at over 4000 tons, double heading of Mendip stone trains is usually with the purpose of repositioning a locomotive rather than satisfying a need for additional pulling power. Such was the case on 29 April 2016 when No. 59005 *Kenneth J Painter* led No. 66094 at the head of the 07.12 Merehead to Acton Yard, seen here approaching Great Bedwyn. Incidentally, during 1991 No. 59005 set a new European haulage record for a single locomotive with a stone train of almost 12,000 tons.

A perfect August morning sees No. 59205 approach Crofton Crossing with loaded Yeoman hoppers forming the 07.12 Merehead Quarry to Acton Yard on 4 August 2014. Prominent in the background is the Crofton Pumping Station, which supplies water to the Savernake summit pound of the Kennet & Avon Canal. The building houses a steam engine installed in 1812, which still operates during certain weekends of the year.

Occasionally engineering work further west requires the overnight loaded oil tanks from Robeston to Theale to be re-timed, allowing the train to be photographed in daylight. On one such occasion the 23.53 departure from Robeston passes Crofton behind No. 60044 *Dowlow* on 4 July 2016. The locomotive was built by Brush Traction at Loughborough during 1991 and originally carried the name *Ailsa Craig* after the island in the Firth of Clyde.

During a perfect summer evening recently re-liveried Class 59/0 No. 59004 *Paul A. Hammond* pass a moored canal narrow boat at Crofton. The train is the 15.24 departure from Acton Yard conveying empty box wagons returning to Merehead Quarry on 18 July 2016.

Overnight frost is only just melting on this crisp late autumn morning as EW&S branded Class 60 No. 60019 *Pathfinder Tours 30 Years of Rail Touring 1973–2003* passes lock 60 at Crofton with a long train of empty Yeoman hoppers from Theale to Merehead Quarry on 10 December 2008.

On a typically hazy spring day No. 43013 leads the (as required) Fridays-only 10.01 Plymouth to London Paddington Network Rail measurement train, seen here passing Crofton pumping station and Wilton Water on 25 March 2011.

No. 43122 drifts around the curve at Crofton leading a London Paddington-bound service on 9 February 2008. On this day Bristol and South Wales services were being diverted via the Berks & Hants. The combination of diversions with the hourly service to and from the South West meant there was a relatively intense train service in operation compared to normal traffic levels along this stretch of line. Unusually this train includes Midland Main Line-liveried trailers, which added some welcome variety to the procession of First Great Western blue HST sets.

On 29 May 2006 Class 37/4 No. 37411 (D6990) *Caerphilly Castle/Castell Caerffili*, finished in British Railways green livery, heads empty stock from Old Oak Common to Plymouth, past Crofton, in advance of working four days of charters on Devon and Cornwall's branch lines in combination with steam locomotive No. 76079. Note the smoke coming from the pumping station chimney.

Hanson Class 59/1 No. 59102 *Village of Chantry* sweeps around the tight curve and past lock 58 at Crofton with the 12.40 Acton Yard to Merehead Quarry on 7 March 2016.

Class 66 No. 66047 has just passed the site of Grafton East Junction whilst heading the Whatley to St Pancras aggregates train on 24 February 2016. The occupation bridge seen here has since been removed.

On 12 February 2005 Class 50 Nos. 50031 *Hood* and 50049 *Defiance* were involved in filming in the Westbury area, believed to be for the BBC. Here *Hood* is seen passing the site of the former Grafton East Junction as it heads back from Westbury to Paddington with a rather mixed rake of coaching stock, with *Defiance* at the rear of the consist. Grafton East Junction consisted of a double-track formation that diverged here running off to the left of this view. It connected the extant Great Western Railway's Berks & Hants route with the long-closed Midland & South Western Junction Railway.

Advenza Freight Class 47 No. 47237 leads three First Great Western Mk 2 coaches past lock 57. Named Adopters Lock, it is dedicated to those who have supported the Kennet & Avon Canal by adopting a stretch of waterway. The train was the 10.10 Laira to Old Oak Common stock move on 16 February 2008. The locomotive has had a fairly uneventful life: built by Brush Traction at Loughborough in 1965 as D1914, it has only carried one number under TOPS.

No. 59004 *Paul A. Hammond*, the then sole surviving Yeoman-liveried Class 59, albeit without logos, has just passed the site of the former Grafton East Junction with the afternoon empty hoppers from Theale Foster Yeoman Stone terminal to Merehead Quarry on 14 May 2014.

With a featherweight load in tow, Class 59/0 No. 59002 *Alan J Day* sweeps through the reverse curves during the ascent to Savernake. The train, consisting of empty Hanson hoppers, originated at Hither Green in South East London and is bound for Whatley Quarry on 4 April 2007.

Paxman Valenta-engined No. 43071 and its London-bound train add a splash of colour to an almost monochrome post-winter scene at the former Wolfhall Junction on 9 March 2006. The power car is about to pass between the abutments of a former overbridge that once carried the Midland & South Western Junction Railway over the GWR's Berks & Hants route. A spur from the M&SWJR joined the latter on the left just before the occupation bridge.

On 10 April 2007 Class 60 No. 60044 passes the site of Wolfhall Junction with the Hither Green to Whatley empty Hanson hoppers. The locomotive is wearing the attractive blue livery, albeit somewhat work-weary, of the former Mainline Freight operation created by British Rail in the years before privatisation. Together with the Load Haul and Transrail operations, Mainline Freight was amalgamated into the English, Welsh & Scottish Railway in 1996, the large logo of which was eventually emblazoned on the body sides of this and many other heritage-liveried Class 60s.

The stylish Class 180 Adelante units had a chequered history with First Great Western. Introduced during 2002, they were moved to pastures new with different operators in 2009 following long-running technical difficulties. Five refurbished units were brought back by FGW in 2012 for use on Cotswold line services, but these have become surplus to requirements with the introduction of the new Hitachi bi-mode trains. No. 180105 is seen here at Wolfhall with an Exeter to London Paddington working on 3 November 2006.

During the afternoon of Saturday 16 February 2008 a work-stained No. 60063 *James Murray* is caught during the final part of the climb to Savernake summit with a Didcot Yard to Westbury loaded spoil train. This train was run in connection with renewal work taking place on the Great Western main line, necessitating the diversion of traffic via the Berks & Hants route.

On a pleasant spring afternoon Hanson Class 59/1 No. 59103 *Village of Mells* and its matching train of hoppers has just passed Savernake summit on 10 April 2007 and is about to run between some hot-box detectors. The train is the regular afternoon departure from Whatley Quarry conveying aggregate to Dagenham in East London.

This is one of the author's favourite Berks & Hants images. It shows Colas Rail Class 60 No. 60076 at the head of the diverted 11.20 Tilbury to Llanwern empty covered steel wagons as the train passes Savernake summit on 18 April 2015. This view was only possible because of recent lineside vegetation clearance by Network Rail, and this happened to coincided with the closure of the Great Western main line for electrification work, necessitating diversion of the train. Near the bridge is the site of the former Savernake Low Level, which served as the junction station for the GWR branch to Marlborough, the trackbed of which can be seen curving away to the left.

Looking in the opposite direction from the previous view and taken four days earlier, No. 59201 approaches Savernake summit from the west with the 10.33 Merehead to Colnbrook. At this point the Kennet & Avon Canal passes under the railway by way of Bruce Tunnel. Behind the locomotive the trackbed of the branch to Marlborough curves away, and the line of trees in the field above the pillbox marks the course of the former Midland & South Western Junction Railway.

The 289-metre Martinsell Hill dominates the background of this view near Burbage Wharf. Class 59/1 No. 59103 *Village of Mells* heads a short set of matching Hanson hopper wagons, en route from Whatley Quarry to Dagenham, during the afternoon of 11 February 2009. It is unfortunate that a radio mast now compromises this view.

The same afternoon saw the unusual sight of loaded Yeoman hoppers heading west past Burbage Wharf bound for Westbury. The train, headed by No. 60060 *James Watt*, was actually a Grain to Theale working conveying sand. All was not well and the train had accumulated considerable delay. The decision was taken to run the train to Westbury and then back to Theale the following day.

By 2016 the appearance of Class 60 locomotives on Mendip stone trains was relatively infrequent. However, during August of that year No. 60017 was to be found working from Westbury. Here the 'tug' heads the 09.04 Merehead Quarry to Theale loaded stone past Brimslade Farm near Wootton Rivers on 12 August 2016.

Reflected in a lineside pool, No. 43161 passes Wootton Rivers on 15 April 2015 whilst leading the 11.33 London Paddington to Exeter St David's.

Approaching a snowy New Mill on 7 February 2009 is EWS-liveried No. 60085 heading the diverted Theale Murco to Margam empty oil tanks.

Class 60 No. 60065 leads failed Class 59/2 No. 59202 at New Mill whilst working the delayed Robeston to Theale loaded Murco oil tanks on 21 April 2009. At this time trials were underway to determine whether Class 59s or pairs of Class 66s could replace Class 60s on this train and a similar working from Robeston to Westerleigh. Ultimately the trials were to prove unsuccessful and, at the time of writing, Class 60s are still employed on these services.

Autumn tints at New Mill and HST power car No. 43185 *Great Western* create a colourful scene on 2 November 2016. The train is the 13.05 London Paddington to Plymouth. The power car is finished in the popular Inter-City 'swallow' livery carried by HSTs during the late 1980s and most of the 1990s.

During the morning of 15 April 2015 Hanson-liveried Class 59/1 No. 59102 *Village of Chantry* was captured having just passed through Pewsey station at the head of the 07.12 Merehead Quarry to Acton Yard, on this occasion formed of a long uniform train of Yeoman hoppers.

Sunshine and showers as Paxman Valenta-engined No. 43132 approaches Manningford Bruce with a westbound service on 20 January 2007. With gentle grades and long sweeping curves the line through the Vale of Pewsey allows drivers to pick up the pace following the curvaceous ascent to Savernake.

Autumnal tints at Woodborough on 18 November 2012. Up and Down loops are provided here to allow freight trains to take refuge while faster passenger services pass. Heading for Westbury, No. 66540 approaches the Down loop with a train of spoil wagons originating from engineering work on the Great Western main line near Reading.

Three Freightliner Class 66 locomotives head this high output ballast train, seen leaving Woodborough Up loop on 20 January 2007. The locomotives are Nos 66530, 66604 and 66529.

The Pewsey Downs are visible in the distance in this view from Beechingstoke of No. 43092 leading the 12.00 London Paddington to Penzance on 5 November 2016.

Looking more like a working from the Derbyshire Peak District than a Mendip stone train, Load Haul-liveried No. 60059 *Swinden Dalesman* and its train of ex-RMC hoppers form the mid-morning departure from Whatley Quarry to St Pancras. The colourful consist is seen passing the former Patney and Chirton station on 21 January 2009. Just beyond here is the former Stert Junction where the original Berks & Hants Extension Railway diverged from the current route and continued to Devizes.

The classic location of Great Cheverell is the setting for this view of No. 59204 *Vale of Glamorgan*, working the afternoon Hither Green to Whatley empty Hanson hoppers, on 19 April 2007. This section of line, known as the Stert & Westbury Railway, was built to create a more direct route from the Berks & Hants line to Westbury for trains running between London and the South West.

A rather faded Transrail-branded Class 60 No. 60061 *Alexander Graham Bell* approaches Great Cheverell with the mid-morning Merehead to Acton aggregates working on 23 January 2009. At the time the Class 60s had fallen out of favour with their operator EWS, and a large proportion of the class were stored. However, during leaf-fall season it was usual for several class members to be brought back into traffic with the purpose of releasing Class 66 locomotives to top and tail rail-head treatment trains. Inevitably Class 60s would find their way onto the Mendip stone circuit where their haulage capabilities could be put to good use. With the leaves having already fallen this Class 60 was on borrowed time.

Freightliner's No. 70015 takes the Basingstoke line at Southcote Junction, Reading. The wide ballasted area to the right of the locomotive and first few wagons marks the site of the junction where the Coley Branch once diverged to serve Reading Central Goods Depot. The branch and depot were opened in 1908 and closed in 1983. The train is the 05.36 departure from Garston in Liverpool to Southampton on 20 April 2016.

This was the Basingstoke branch of the Berks & Hants Railway, now forming an important north–south link for long-distance freight and passenger services. Intermodal services to and from Southampton dominate the freight scene. Providing a welcome change during the evening of 23 April 2010 is No. 60096 as it approaches Mortimer with a Scunthorpe to Eastleigh Yard working conveying new rails. At the time Class 60s were few and far between. With only a handful in service, it was more usual to find them employed on heavy oil trains working from South Wales or Immingham.

During recent years the two prototype Class 150 DMU Nos. 150001 and 150002 have been employed on the shuttle services between Reading and Basingstoke. In wonderful evening light on 29 April 2015 No. 150001 is seen to the south of Mortimer near Silchester forming the 17.08 departure from Reading.

On 3 February 2007 No. 66192 and its train of covered car carriers snakes away from the South Western main line at Basingstoke and takes the line to Reading. These wagons are a common sight working between the Southampton docks, Oxford, the Midlands and the North West.

Frost still lies in the shadowed areas as veteran Class 47 No. 47815 passes the 1966-built signal box on the South Western main line at Basingstoke, with Class 442 unit Nos 2424 and 2405 in tow. The train is the 07.52 Ely Papworth Sidings to Eastleigh Works (Arlington). No. 47815 entered traffic in 1964 as D1748, was renumbered to 47155 in December 1973, became 47660 in December 1986, before finally becoming 47815 in August 1989. (Photograph by Trevor Maxted)

South West Trains Class 159/0 No. 159003 passes the cottages at Worting Junction to the west of Basingstoke, forming a West of England service from London Waterloo to Salisbury on 3 February 2007. These units took over from locomotive-hauled trains on the Waterloo to Salisbury and Exeter services during 1993. No. 159003 was part of the first batch of twenty-two units that were converted from Class 158s.

On 3 February 2007 Virgin CrossCountry Super Voyager No. 221106 passes Battledown flyover, just to the west of Worting Junction. Here the West of England line to Salisbury and Exeter diverges from the South Western main line. The Voyager is taking the latter, forming a service bound for the south coast. At this time the Virgin franchise had only around nine months to run before Arriva took over the cross-country network.

Standing in for the usual Class 66, Class 37/4 No. 37417 *Richard Trevithick* passes Whitchurch station on 7 July 2008 heading a lightly loaded Southampton Western Docks to Bescot automotive working. (Photograph by Richard Sulzmann)

A large number of former BR Southern Region Mk 1 EMUs were taken to Caerwent in South Wales for scrapping. Usually these trains were routed via the Great Western main line. However, on 14 April 2005 No. 47830 with unit numbers 3405 and 3456 were routed via Salisbury and Westbury. The ensemble is seen crossing Hurstbourne Viaduct just to the east of Andover.

The railway between Reading and Didcot through the Thames Valley is part of Brunel's original London to Bristol route. Here Class 60 No. 60059 *Swinden Dalesman* passes through the recently cleared cutting at Purley-on-Thames in charge of the empty oil tanks from Theale to Robeston in South West Wales on 6 April 2006. The locomotive is wearing the then obsolete Load Haul livery. Load Haul was one of the freight entities set up by British Rail during the run up to privatisation. English, Welsh & Scottish Railway took over operation of Load Haul but some locomotives, including this example, retained the orange and black livery for several years after.

An unusual working through the Thames Valley on 4 May 2006 was this movement of redundant First Great Western Motorail stock from Old Oak Common for storage at Long Marston, seen here having just passed through Pangbourne station led by Class 66 No. 66229. The Motorail brand was introduced by BR in 1966 and lasted until 1995. First Great Western reintroduced the brand in 1999 on some services between London Paddington and Penzance but this ceased during 2005.

On 21 September 2006 Freightliner Class 66 No. 66575 passes through the deep chalk cutting on the approach to Pangbourne with a Southampton-bound intermodal working. Intermodals dominate freight movements through the Thames Valley, between terminals in the North of England, the Midlands, South Wales and Southampton, and between Bristol and London Gateway.

During the afternoon of 6 April 2006 Class 66 No. 66130 passes Lower Basildon with loaded bitumen tanks on their way from Fawley Refinery, near Southampton, to Bromford Bridge in the West Midlands. All rail traffic from Fawley ceased during 2016, but this particular flow was withdrawn in 2009.

Seen before it received its unique blue livery, Class 60 No. 60074 passes Lower Basildon with an additional working of aggregate from Moreton-on-Lugg to Hayes carried in two-axle Gunnel wagons on 17 November 2005. The road bridge was replaced with a modern single-span structure as part of the preparation for electrification.

The long summer evening of 30 June 2004 sees Class 57/0 No. 57004 *Freightliner Quality* on the Up relief line at Lower Basildon between Goring and Pangbourne. Twelve Class 57/0s were created by re-engineering redundant Class 47s, initially leased by Porterbrook and operated by Freightliner. The first locomotive entered traffic during 1998, but by 2007 they had started to be replaced by Class 66s. Since then all twelve have found homes with other operators, No. 57004 with Direct Rail Services.

The Sundays-only Didcot to Colnbrook oil terminal was an infrequent runner, but increased demand for aviation fuel at Heathrow during summer months saw the train run almost weekly for short periods. The train originated from the Lindsey refinery and, unlike the regular weekday workings to Colnbrook, it spent the night in Didcot Yard, rather than use the more direct route via the Midland main line. Seen from the edge of the Chiltern Hills 6A70, the 08.32 departure from Didcot, passes through the scenic Goring Gap and crosses the River Thames headed by No. 60007 on 13 May 2012.

Cross-country services operate through the Thames Valley between Bournemouth, Southampton and Reading to Newcastle and Manchester, with one service in each direction extending beyond Reading to Guildford. The Class 220 and 221 Voyager units were in charge of these services throughout the period covered. Arriva Class 220 No. 220015 passes Spring Farm, Goring, during the evening of 9 May 2014 whilst working a northbound service.

On 9 May 2014 Freightliner Class 70 No. 70009 passes Spring Farm, Goring, with the well-loaded 11.52 Crewe to Southampton intermodal. The Class 70s were built by General Electric in Pennsylvania, and the first locomotives arrived in the UK during 2009. In recent years a large proportion of Freightliner Class 70 fleet have spent a significant time in storage.

No. 60040 *The Territorial Army Centenary* and its train of empty oil tanks from Theale to Robeston are on the Down fast line as they cross the Thames on Five Arches Bridge at Moulsford on 2 January 2015.

Local passenger services in the Thames Valley were worked exclusively by Class 165 and 166 'Turbos' since the units' introduction during the 1990s, until electric services started in 2018. Class 166 DMU No. 166204 has just crossed the River Thames at Moulsford whilst working a London Paddington to Oxford stopping service on 2 October 2004. In January 2018 Class 387 EMUs took over these services, terminating Didcot Parkway.

UK Rail Leasing Class 56 locomotives Nos 56104 and 56081 top and tail two barrier vehicles as they pass the site of the former Wallingford Road station, en route from Eastleigh to Tyseley, on 10 September 2015. In 1866 Wallingford Road was renamed Moulsford when the Wallingford branch, which had its junction with the main line at the station, was opened. Moulsford station closed in 1892 with the quadrupling of the main line, when the branch junction was resited at what is now Cholsey station. However, the former station building, seen here, has been retained as a private residence.

Seen from high above the cutting between Moulsford and Cholsey, Class 66 No. 66056 heads a train of northbound car carriers from Southampton along the down relief line on 3 June 2010. The Chiltern escarpment is prominent in the background.

The long-distance workings between London Paddington, Bristol and South Wales were the first to see HSTs when they were introduced to the Western Region of British Rail in 1976. No. 43022 has just passed through Cholsey station with a London-bound express on 16 April 2014. On the horizon are the Didcot power stations, a prominent local landmark. The coal-fired Didcot A power station had closed just over a year before, during March 2013. Later in 2014 the southernmost group of cooling towers were demolished.

A Class 166 departs from Cholsey forming a stopping service to Oxford during the evening of 5 April 2007. St Mary's Church peeps over the railway embankment. Dating back to the tenth century, the church's most well-known member was crime-writer Agatha Christie, who is buried in the churchyard.

On 18 March 2005 Class 37/4 No. 37427 made a welcome change from the normal Class 66 at the head of the afternoon Eastleigh Yard to Hinksey Yard engineers' working. On this occasion the train consisted of long welded rail carriers, seen here passing Cholsey in fine early spring sunshine.

One of the hazards of photographing intermodal workings is the chance that the train will be mainly transporting fresh air. At around 06.30 on 2 June 2006 Class 57/0 No. 57001 *Freightliner Pioneer* was in charge of such a duty when it was captured passing Cholsey at the head of the daily Southampton to Cardiff Wentloog working.

Network Rail's Laboratory 19, an ex-Class 101 power twin renumbered to No. 901002 and named *Iris 2*, scurries along the Up main line at Cholsey Manor Farm on 6 March 2003 en route from Derby Railway Technical Centre to Fratton. In this form the unit was used for radio and video survey work.

Superb evening light illuminates Colas Rail Freight Class 56 No. 56302 as it leads the heavily delayed Tilbury to Llanwern empty covered steel carriers at Cholsey Manor Farm on 22 March 2014. The locomotive was built at Crewe Works during 1983 and numbered 56124. It was renumbered in 2006 when it was overhauled by Brush Traction for the freight operator Fastline.

The oil terminal at Theale near Reading received trains from Robeston in South West Wales and Lindsey in Lincolnshire. Class 60 No. 60025 *Caledonian Paper* has charge of a train of empties returning from Theale to Lindsey, seen passing South Moreton on 26 March 2007.

Power car No. 43017 was built at Crewe during 1976 and paired with No. 43016 to form set No. 253008, which was part of the original batch of trains delivered to the Western Region of British Rail. Seen in its original home territory some thirty-four years on, having come off the Oxford line Paddington bound, No. 43017 crosses to the Up main at Didcot East on 9 January 2010.

During the evening of 9 December 2004 Load Haul-liveried Class 37 No. 37710 stands in the sidings adjacent to Didcot Parkway station with a set of rail head treatment wagons and Classmate No. 37798 at the rear. The ensemble would soon venture into the night to cleanse the rails of residue from fallen leaves, ready for services to begin again the following morning

Non-standard liveried Class 37/5 No. 37692, unofficially named *Didcot Depot*, rests in Didcot Yard with rail-head treatment wagons and classmate No. 37174 on 7 October 2004. No. D6822 was built by Robert Stephenson & Hawthorn Ltd at Darlington during 1963. Under TOPS it was renumbered to No. 37122, before being renumbered once more during overhaul at Crewe Works in 1987.

By 2013 opportunities to photograph EWS-liveried Class 60s were becoming increasingly rare as DBS introduced refurbished examples in their bright red livery. On 29 October No. 60049, with original EW&S lettering, passes Didcot Parkway with the 13.00 Theale to Robeston empty Murco oil tanks.

During the evening of 14 March 2005 FM Rail Class 33/1 No. 33103 *Swordfish* propels observation saloon No. 975025 Caroline into the Great Western Society's Didcot Railway Centre. The observation saloon was built in 1958 as a buffet car for a Class 203 Hastings Unit, which explains its narrow body profile. During 1969 it was converted to become the Southern Region General Manager's Saloon and fitted with equipment to allow it to work in push-pull operation with Class 33 and 73 locomotives.

On occasions main line registered diesel locomotives are stabled between duties within the confines of the Didcot Railway Centre. Here Class 31/4 No. 31454 *The Heart of Wessex*, operated by spot-hire company FM Rail, rests next to the locomotive shed on 24 April 2005.

Stored at the back of Didcot yard are Class 08 Nos 08856 and 08913 bask in morning sunshine on 29 May 2005. Once common in freight yards, carriage sidings and at large stations, these dedicated shunting locomotives have become few and far between. Most marshalling of freight trains is now carried out by main line locomotives, and passenger train consists are predominantly fixed-formation units that are only spilt up when maintenance is required.

On 14 March 2013, only a couple of weeks before the closure of Didcot A power station, No. 66169 runs around its train of EWS empty coal hoppers at Foxhall Junction, before returning to Avonmouth to reload with more imported coal. By this time stockpiles of coal at Didcot had been run down and the power station was reliant on new deliveries by rail.

On 4 March 2013 DCR Class 56 No. 56303 (ex 56125) has just come off Didcot West Curve at Foxhall Junction and is taking the line into Didcot power station with empty box wagons from Calvert. These will be loaded with fly ash, a product of coal combustion that is sometimes used by the construction industry in concrete production.

On 5 April 2006 No. 60071 is caught easing its train of empty oil tanks out of the sidings at the Didcot power stations. The train is bound for Lindsey Oil Refinery in Lincolnshire. The cooling towers are part of Didcot A power station, which was a combined coal and oil plant, later converted to co-fire with gas, and had a capacity of 2 GW. Didcot A ceased operation on 22 March 2013, some forty-five years after opening. The small chimney on the left is part of the 1.3 GW gas-fired Didcot B, which opened in 1997 and is still operational today.

21 January 2009 saw blue-liveried Class 60 No. 60074 work the Theale to Robeston empty Murco oil tanks. The train is illuminated by winter sunlight as it passes Milton Park. The land to the right of the train has since been developed.

Didcot power stations A and B dominate the background as EWS Class 66 No. 66036 approaches Steventon with empty HTA coal hoppers bound for Avonmouth on 18 November 2005.

Looking westwards from the road bridge at Steventon on 16 April 2006, we see Class 66/6 No. 66606 approaching with the 10.05 from Thingley Junction, formed of high output ballast hoppers returning from an overnight worksite to Reading West Junction Yard. Network Rail's high output ballast cleaner system automatically screens and removes worn ballast and adds new chippings where necessary. With these trains renewal work that used to take a whole weekend using traditional methods can be completed overnight.

On 24 February 2016 Class 56 No. 56104 is captured heading west through Steventon with a very light load in tow. It is conveying a single Chiltern Railways Mk 3 coach from Wembley to Bristol Barton Hill depot for refurbishment. There used to be a station here and, for a short time during the line's construction, it became the temporary headquarters of the Great Western Railway due to its location roughly midway between London and Bristol. Note the white painted area on the bridge that was once intended to aid drivers with the sighting of semaphore signals.

Low autumnal sunlight illuminates No. 56087 as it heads the 11.20 departure from Tilbury to Llanwern, consisting of empty covered steel carriers. The remains of the closed Didcot A power station including the 200-metre-high chimney are prominent in the background. The plume of steam originates from the still active Didcot B.

Following the mass withdrawal of slam-door rolling stock from South West Trains and Connex South Central services there were numerous stock moves to Caerwent in South Wales where the units were scrapped. With threatening skies over Didcot power stations, First Great Western Class 57/6 No. 57604 *Pendennis Castle* heads west near Steventon, with Connex-liveried units in tow, on 28 February 2006.

Up and Down relief lines are provided between the sites of the former Wantage Road and Challow stations to allow passenger services to pass freight trains. The village of Denchworth lies roughly midway along this quadrupled section, and Circourt Bridge was once a popular location for photographers, providing uninterrupted views in both directions. Taking the Down main, Freightliner Class 66 No. 66954 speeds westwards with a well-loaded Southampton to Wentloog intermodal on 2 November 2012.

Looking in the opposite direction on 17 November 2005, EWS Class 66 No. 66233 passes Denchworth conveying military vehicles from the MOD storage site at Ashchurch, near Tewkesbury, to Didcot Yard.

Autumnal sunlight highlights No. 67026 *Diamond Jubilee* as it approaches Circourt Bridge on 30 November 2014 with Pullman stock forming the 12.16 charter from Chippenham to London Victoria.

On 16 December 2012 West Coast Railways Class 47/4 No. 47500 leads No. 34067 *Tangmere* at the head of empty stock running from Bristol Kingsland Road to Southall, seen here passing the site of Challow station. D1943 was built by Brush Traction at Loughborough during 1966, and was renumbered to 47500 under TOPS and named *Great Western* during 1979. The locomotive was repainted in Brunswick green for the GWR150 celebrations in 1985. During 1995 it was renumbered to 47770 when the locomotive was part of the Rail Express Systems fleet, regaining its original TOPS number in 2010.

The freight operator Fastline had a small fleet of Class 56 and Class 66 locomotives. The company ceased trading in 2010 when owners Jarvis went into administration. Captured during the relatively short period when Fastline operated coal trains, on 3 January 2009 No. 66301 heads east at Baulking with imported coal from the docks at Avonmouth, bound for Ratcliffe power station.

During 2008 Class 60 No. 60040 was finished in a non-standard red livery and named *The Territorial Army Centenary*. The locomotive is seen near Baulking on 3 December 2008 whilst returning empty aggregate box wagons from Oxford Banbury Road to the Mendips.

On 28 March 2005 No. 66073 passes Uffington with the diverted Mondays-only Tavistock Junction Yard to Dollands Moor. The train is conveying china clay for export through the Channel Tunnel and would normally be routed via the Berks & Hants. The first three wagons carry bagged clay and the remainder of the consist is carrying bulk powder in hoppers.

On 3 May 2016 the 07.55 Westbury to Bescot engineers passes Ruffinswick Farm, near Compton Beauchamp, behind Colas Rail Class 70 No. 70805. The arches in the road bridge and the former trackbed seen to the right of the locomotive give away the fact that there was once an additional Up line here. A long loop ran from Shrivenham in the west to as far as Knighton Crossing in the east.

A light covering of snow during the night, and clear skies the following morning, created perfect conditions to record No. 67020 heading the 08.25 Cardiff Central to London Paddington football extra. Typically for charter trains in recent years, the stock carries a variety of liveries. The colourful combination passes Ruffinswick Farm on 6 April 2008.

For a relatively short period Colas Rail Freight operated steel trains between South Wales at Tilbury. These trains featured a variety of motive power including Classes 56 and 66 before their then recently acquired fleet of Class 60 locomotives became regular traction. The loaded trains from Wales often ran overnight, but the return empties would usually run during the following day. Passing what was probably the most pleasant location on the section between Didcot and Swindon, at Ruffinswick Farm, is No. 60087 with the 11.20 departure from Tilbury Riverside to Llanwern on 25 October 2014.

BR blue-liveried Class 47/4 No. 47840 *North Star* approaches Shrivenham with a stock move conveying refurbished HST buffet cars, from Old Oak Common to Plymouth Laira, on 17 March 2007. D1661 was a product of Crewe Works during 1965. It was renumbered to 47077 under TOPS and again to 47613 when ETS equipment was fitted. It joined the extended range fleet during 1989 and was renumbered in the 478xx series. The locomotive first carried the name *North Star* in 1965 and has had a long association with the Western Region of BR.

Freightliner Class 66 No. 66549 heads empty refuse containers from the landfill site at Calvert in Buckinghamshire to waste transfer stations at Bath Oldfield Park and Bristol Lawrence Hill for loading. The train, which no longer runs, was known as the 'binliner' and is seen approaching the former station at Shrivenham on 1 November 2006.

During the weekends of the 18/19 and 25/26 April 2015 work was undertaken at Bourton, east of Swindon, to lower the trackbed of the Great Western main line. The reason for this work was to allow two listed overbridges (of limited clearance) to be retained during the forthcoming electrification of the line. One of the listed bridges, Steppingstone Lane, is seen here. No. 66850 ticks over on the already realigned Up line whilst its train is loaded with spoil from the lifted Down line. The locomotive originally entered traffic with Freightliner in 2004 as No. 66577. It was subsequently renumbered and transferred to Colas during 2011.

Following the end of the 'binliner' service from Calvert to Bath and Bristol there was a period of several years when the Great Western main line, west of Didcot, was devoid of such traffic. This changed with the introduction of a flow of waste between West London and a new energy recovery centre adjacent to the Severn Beach branch. On 25 September 2016 No. 66015 heads west past Bourton with the 13.11 departure from Southall Yard conveying loaded wagons.

The low-angled winter sunlight gives a deceptively warm glow to this bitterly cold January day. Freightliner Class 66 No. 66569 passes Bourton with a well-loaded, but very late running, Wentloog to Southampton intermodal service on 7 January 2010.

This scene, recorded at Highworth Junction on 14 May 2014, shows Freightliner's No. 66594 coming off the Up main and into Stratton loop with a rather sparsely loaded intermodal working. Meanwhile EWS-liveried No. 66023 and its MBA wagons loaded with scrap metal sit on the remains of the old Highworth branch. Following closure of the branch in 1962 a small section was retained to serve the nearby automotive factories. The sidings in the distance on the left were being used for the servicing of specialist on-track plant in connection with the Great Western main line electrification project.

First Great Western green-liveried No. 43188 pauses at Swindon at the head of an evening westbound service from London Paddington on 7 September 2004. Note the contrast in architecture on the Up and Down sides of the station – the modern office block being erected during the early 1970s on the site of the original main station building.

During the wet evening of 17 January 2005 Wessex Trains Class 150 No. 150239 rests in the bay platform at the west end of Swindon station. These units were used on services from Swindon to Gloucester, via the Golden Valley, and to Westbury, via Chippenham and Melksham. Wessex Trains services were subsumed into the Greater Western franchise in 2006.

No. 43156 arrives at Swindon, with the 09.00 Bristol Temple Meads to London Paddington in tow, on a hazy 15 September 2016. The train is passing the remains of the former Great Western Railway workshops, some of which have been converted into residential and commercial units.

Apart from engineering trains, during this period very few freight services were formed of two-axle wagons. Freightliner Class 66/6 No. 66604 heads a uniform set of empty PGA hopper wagons from Angerstein Wharf to Cardiff Pengam. The train is approaching Brinkworth on the line from Wootton Bassett Junction to Bristol Parkway on 7 October 2006.

A regular Freightliner Class 57 working used to be the daily Southampton Maritime to Cardiff Wentloog and return. Quite often the first few wagons of the return working ran empty, so it was pleasing to record the train with a fully loaded consist behind No. 57012 *Freightliner Envoy*, passing Brinkworth on 9 November 2006.

The Northern Belle from Gobowen to Bath Spa, on 8 September 2012, passes Langley Burrell near Chippenham with Direct Rail Services Class 47/4 No. 47832 *Solway Princess* in charge. No. D1610 was built in 1964 at Crewe Works. It was renumbered to No. 47031 under TOPS in 1973 and renumbered again to No. 47560 in 1980 when it was fitted with ETS. During 1989 it joined the long-range locomotives numbered in the 478xx series.

Freightliner Class 66 No. 66542 creeps around the curve from Didcot North Junction to Didcot Parkway station with a well-loaded intermodal on 7 March 2014. Freight is sometimes routed via the station to allow passenger services to pass on the Didcot avoider or to allow a crew change.

Romanian-built Class 56 No. 56312 (formerly No. 56003) creeps around the West Curve at Didcot with the Calvert to Didcot power station empty fly ash wagons on 7 November 2012. The train is passing Network Rail's Thames Valley Signalling Centre, which opened during 2010 and has gradually replaced panel signal boxes in the Thames Valley area and beyond.

On 21 April 2018, Locomotive Services Limited Class 47 No. 47501 (D1944) *Craftsman*, finished in British Railways two-tone green, leaves the Didcot avoider at the head of the 03.59 Crewe to Oxford ECS. The train would continue from Oxford as a charter, heading north to Crewe and onwards to Chester, the latter leg of the journey using steam traction. Classmate No. 47805, also in green, can be seen at the rear of the consist.

A new livery to appear in 2019 was the DB/Martime Transport blue scheme, seen here worn by No. 66005 while approaching Didcot North Junction on 1 June. The train is the 04.11 from Wakefield Europort to Didcot Yard, which is often poorly loaded. The white building (top right) is at the Culham Science Centre, home to the European JET Facility, the largest nuclear fusion research machine.

Network Rail Class 43 No. 43062 has just crossed the River Thames at Appleford whilst working the 16.13 Derby to Old Oak Common New Measurement Train on 13 May 2015.

Early morning spring sunshine on 17 April 2006 illuminates Virgin CrossCountry Class 221 Super Voyager No. 221133 as it heads north near Culham. These diesel-electric units were built with a tilting mechanism to allow faster speeds on curving track. However, the cross-country units have had this mechanism disabled to increase reliability, since most of their routes are not cleared for tilting trains.

Not long before sunset, on 29 May 2015, Class 66 No. 66116 has just got into its stride as it approaches Culham station with the 20.28 Didcot Yard to Mossend. Although on this particular occasion the consist is formed mainly of car carriers, this train is one of the few mixed freight workings left on the network. The sharp eyed will spot two HEA hoppers at the rear of the train, which were conveying aggregates for a well-known DIY chain.

Cotswold Rail-liveried Class 47/4 No. 47813 heads Blue Pullman stock at Culham during the evening of 5 May 2007. Founded in 2000, Cotswold Rail was a spot hire company that operated until 2009. The locomotive entered traffic during 1964 as D1720, becoming No. 47129 under TOPS. During 1986 it was renumbered to No. 47658 when it was fitted with ETS equipment and extended-range fuel tanks. In 1989 it was renumbered again as No. 47813, when it was decided to create a new 478xx number series for longer-range locomotives.

Freightliner Class 66/6 No. 66611 heads a short high output ballast train through Culham during the evening of 5 May 2007. The chalk ridge of Berkshire Downs forms the distant backdrop.

Devon & Cornwall Railways No. 56311 approaches Kennington Junction with the 10.53 Calvert to Didcot power station empty fly ash wagons on 18 February 2013. The ash is a waste product from the combustion of coal that has uses in the construction industry. Later the same day the train would be reloaded at the power station before returning to Buckinghamshire, where the material was being used in the building of an incinerator. The southern end of Hinksey Yard can be seen in the background.

It is the Easter weekend and Hinksey Yard is well stocked with engineering wagons of varying vintages, including seacows and auto-ballasters. Resident Class 08 No. 08676 rests between shunting duties on 26 March 2005.

On 6 October 2012 veteran Class 31/1 No. 31106 passes Hinksey Yard at the head of the 13.57 Eastleigh to Derby RTC Network Rail test train. During its long career the locomotive has only carried two numbers, emerging from Brush Traction's Loughborough works during 1959 as No. D5524.

A nationwide network of timetabled engineers' trains allows equipment and materials to be moved around the country to where they are required for planned overnight or weekend possessions. Late afternoon on 13 October 2010 sees No. 60048 arrive at Hinksey Yard with the daily working from Eastleigh. The locomotive is slowly drawing a lengthy train through the virtual quarry sidings to allow it to set back into the main part of the yard.

For many years Didcot was a hub for MOD rail traffic, with regular workings to and from Ashchurch, Kineton, Ludgershall, Marchwood and Bicester. On 6 October 2010 Class 60 No. 60071 *Ribblehead Viaduct* passes Hinksey Lake with an afternoon working from the latter to Didcot.

Direct Rail Services Class 37/4 Nos. 37401 *Mary Queen of Scots* and 37405 approach Oxford with 'The Bournemouth Flyer' charter, the 06.17 departure from Chester, on 14 August 2014. The lead locomotive is wearing the attractive BR large logo blue livery, a reminder of its days working from Glasgow's Eastfield depot.

Class 56 Nos. 56301 (ex 56045) and 56312 (ex 56003) pass the old Oxford Banbury Road aggregates terminal with empty box wagons from Calvert to Didcot power station on 12 December 2012. This is now the site of Oxford Parkway station, which opened in 2015.

During the evening of 26 June 2018 DRS Class 68 No. 68009 leads the 18.18 London Marylebone to Oxford Chiltern Railways service at Oddington. This section of line between Bicester and Oxford has seen a new lease of life following significant work to restore double track for the introduction of these new services from Marylebone to Oxford Parkway and Oxford.

Earlier the same evening Great Western Railway No. 43004 leads the 17.22 London Paddington to Hereford at Cassington near the start of the single line section from Wolvercote Junction to Charlbury on the Cotswold line. At the time the use of HSTs on Cotswold services was drawing to a close as IETs were phased in. The white building seen above the bridge is Oxford's John Radcliffe Hospital.

Also available from Amberley Publishing

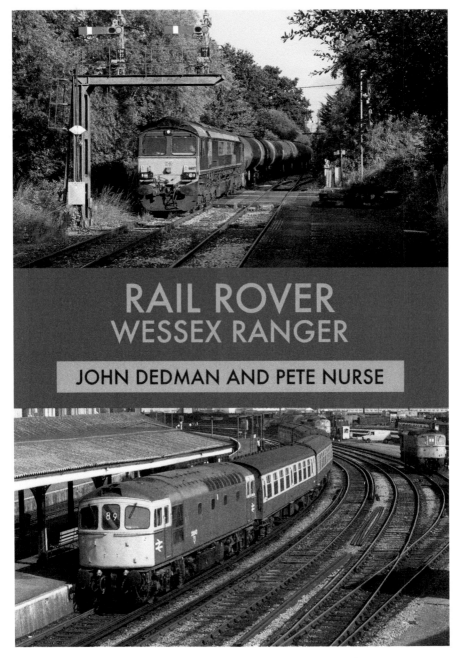

RAIL ROVER
WESSEX RANGER

JOHN DEDMAN AND PETE NURSE